Andrew Dickson White

The Greater States of Continental Europe

Syllabus Prepared for the Graduating Classes of the Cornell University

Andrew Dickson White

The Greater States of Continental Europe
Syllabus Prepared for the Graduating Classes of the Cornell University

ISBN/EAN: 9783337403973

Printed in Europe, USA, Canada, Australia, Japan

Cover: Foto ©Suzi / pixelio.de

More available books at **www.hansebooks.com**

ANALYSIS OF LECTURES

ON THE GREATER STATES OF

CONTINENTAL EUROPE.

BY

ANDREW D. WHITE.

THE GREATER STATES

OF

CONTINENTAL EUROPE:

SYLLABUS

PREPARED FOR THE GRADUATING CLASSES

OF

THE CORNELL UNIVERSITY.

BY ANDREW D. WHITE,

PRESIDENT, AND PROFESSOR OF HISTORY.

TO THE

Reverend Noah Porter, D. D.,

PRESIDENT OF YALE COLLEGE,

IN GRATITUDE FOR INSTRUCTION AND FRIENDSHIP,

I DEDICATE

THIS COURSE OF LECTURES.

A. D. W.

Cornell University, April, 1874.

SYLLABUS.

ITALY.
FIRST LECTURE.

FROM DESTRUCTION OF HER INDEPENDENCE BY CHARLES V.
(1530) *TO FRENCH REVOLUTION* (1789).

1. END OF THE ITALIAN REPUBLIC AND REPUBLICAN
LIBERTIES. Want of Civil Liberty. Intense local spirit.
Anarchy. Two causes of Foreign Intervention.

2. FINAL BLOW TO ITALIAN LIBERTY AND INDEPEND-
ENCE. Charles V.; his coronation at Bologna, February,
1530. Ferruci's struggle.

3. GENERAL SUMMARY OF ITALIAN HISTORY FROM THE
LOSS OF INDEPENDENCE TO THE FRENCH REVOLUTION.

Divisions in territory ;—in political action and feeling.

Civil War between rival territories, as Genoa and Corsica ;
between rival houses, as Barberini and Farnese ; between rival factions, as the Inscribed and Uninscribed nobles of Genoa.

Insurrections of mobs, as of Masaniello at Naples : insurrections headed by schemers, as of Fiesco at Genoa : insurrections headed by patriots, as of Burlamacchi at Lucca.

Tyranny and Luxury, as of the Gonzaga, Este and other
reigning families.

Plots and Assassinations. Assassination of Alexander by Lorenzino de Medicis as a type.

Oppression by Foreign Powers. Louis XIV. and his brutal methods, as towards Genoa. Austria, and the growth of her influence. The one bright spot. The Leopoldine Administration in Tuscany.

4. THE PAPACY. Revival of its earnestness and devotion to Religion at close of Sixteenth Century. Paul IV. and the Inquisition. Pius V. and the present to the Duke of Alva. Papal league with the Jesuits. Education. Papal Government and its defects. The great Pope, Sixtus V.

ITALY.

SECOND LECTURE.

FROM 1530 TO 1789—CONTINUED.

1. DECLINE IN THE ITALIAN CHARACTER.   Political atrophy.   Moral, social and religious debasement.   Two great causes and consequences of this: I. Substitution of Spanish for Italian ideas of labor; II. Cicisbeism and loss of family life.   Italian education of that period.   General characteristics of the Sixteenth Century revealed in Benvenuto Cellini's Memoirs.

2. DECLINE IN SCIENCE AND LITERATURE.   Rise of great men, and their reception.   Galileo and Giannone.   Course of literature.   Metastasio.   Alfieri.

3. DECLINE OF ART.   Painting.   Sculpture.   Architecture.

4. PRESERVATION OF NOMINAL REPUBLICS; Venice as typical.

5. THE HOUSE OF SAVOY.   Its bad and good qualities.

6. REVIVAL OF THOUGHT, and especially in the Eighteenth Century.   Vico.   Beccaria.   Filangieri.   Deadness. of the Italian peninsula at the outbreak of the French Revolution.

ITALY.

THIRD LECTURE.

FROM 1789 TO 1815.

1. IDEAS OF BARTOLI just before 1786 as to the impossibility of further revolutions in Italy.

2. EFFECTS OF FRENCH THOUGHT. Effects of reforms of Leopold and others. Difference between upper and lower classes in reception of the new ideas.

3. CHECK UPON ADVANCE OF REVOLUTION IN ITALY by French extravagance and terrorism.

4. BONAPARTE'S APOSTOLATE for liberty in Italy. His qualifications. His method of securing the coöperation of Italian liberals. Comparisons between various proclamations of Bonaparte at this period. Effects of his victories.

5. THE NEW ITALIAN REPUBLICS. Causes of Italian estrangement from the French. Culmination in Treaty of Campo Formio.

6. FALLING BACK OF ITALY during Bonaparte's absence in Egypt. Effect of his return. Passage of the Alps. Battle of Marengo.

7. HIS FATAL DEALINGS WITH ITALIAN UNITY. Apparent exception in consolidation in Northern Italy. His management with Naples and Tuscany as showing his real spirit.

8. HIS FATAL DEALINGS WITH ITALIAN LIBERTY. Transformation of republics into kingdoms. Provision for his family and retainers in them. Suffering and loss of Italy, under him, in men, in treasure, and in monuments. One redeeming feature. Improvement in administration.

9. REACTION IN ITALY AFTER DOWNFALL OF NAPOLEON. State of Italian feeling. Dealings with Italy by the allied powers. Establishment in the peninsula of Austrian supremacy.

10. FUTILITY OF THE SETTLEMENT OF ITALIAN AFFAIRS at the Restoration of the Bourbons. Violation of the national feelings for liberty, unity and independence,

ITALY.

FOURTH LECTURE.

FROM 1815 TO 1848.

1. RISE AND PROGRESS OF LIBERALISM. Growth of secret societies. The Carbonari (Ventes, Bons Cousins, etc.)

2. FARTHER ENCROACHMENTS OF REACTION. Meeting of European sovereigns at Aix-la-Chapelle, Troppau, etc. Reëstablishment of the Jesuits by Pope Pius. Reactionary writings. De Maistre. Reactionary secret societies. The Sanfediste. Constitutions withdrawn. Efforts to keep down intelligence. Discrimination against foreign books in Naples.

3. DISHEARTENING EVENTS FOR ITALIAN LIBERALS. Attempted revolution of 1821 ; its failure ; wretched part taken by Charles Albert in it. Political effect of the cholera. Despotism triumphant. Typical case of Enrico Mayer.

4. TWO NEW GROWTHS OF LIBERALISM : A. The Radicals. Joseph Mazzini ; his early education ; his reasons for casting aside Carbonarism. Creation of the Young Italy Party. Mode of working. Sad results ; case of the Bandieri as typical. B. The Moderates and their work.

ITALY.

FIFTH LECTURE.

FROM 1815 TO 1848—CONTINUED.

1. THE MODERATE REFORMERS AND THEIR WORK.
Completion of the *History of the Italian Republic*, by Sis-
mondi (1818); character of its final chapters. Cesare Bàlbo,
and his work on *The Hopes of Italy*. Vincenzo Gioberti, and
his work on *The Primacy of Italy*. Massimo d' Azeglio, and
his writings, especially the *Ultimi casi di Romagna*. Giuseppe
Giusti, and his poems.

2. ANARCHIC TENDENCIES. Struggles and quarrels. Italian journalism, and its miserable part in these struggles.

3. ACCESSION OF PIUS IX. TO THE PAPACY. Noble elements in his character. Hopes of the liberals. Reforms by
Pius. His caution and halting. Way in which his efforts
were met. Assassination of Rossi. (One effect of political
assassinations). Flight of the Pope. His reëstablishment
by the French. Destruction of the Roman Republic.

4. CHARLES ALBERT, KING OF PIEDMONT. Hope of Moderate party in him. Characteristics of his family; value of
these. Charles Albert at the head of a new movement for
independence. Defeat at Novara. Abdication and death of
king. Accession of Victor Emanuel.

5. PROSTRATION OF ITALY. Cruelties at the sacking of
Brescia. Severities at Milan. General harshness of Austrian
rule in Italy. Bigotry and reaction triumphant.

ITALY.

SIXTH LECTURE.

CAVOUR, VICTOR EMANUEL AND THE NEW KINGDOM.

1. RECAPITULATION OF ITALIAN AFFAIRS up to 1849.

2. CONDUCT OF VICTOR EMANUEL at his accession. Radetzky's proposal as to violation of the Constitution. Victor Emanuel's answer and its cost.

3. CHARACTERISTICS OF SAVOY; its people; its ruling house. Its bigotry in former days; its basis of truthfulness and steadiness; recent examples in the Spanish branch of the House of Savoy (1872–3).

4. FIRST MINISTRY. D' Azeglio and others.

5. CAVOUR; his education; his early history; his conduct of Sardinian affairs under Victor Emanuel; his policy as to the Crimean War; his struggle at Paris.

6. THE WAR OF 1859 WITH AUSTRIA. Causes which led France into it. Personal and political causes; the Orsini attempt in Paris (January 14, 1858). Edmond About's *Roman Question*. Battles of Magenta and Solferino and their results. Peace of Villa Franca. Cession of Nice and Savoy to France. Moral effect of this in Italy. Garibaldi at Naples. Kingdom of Italy founded. Death of Cavour, 1861. His last words. Fitting monument to him in the Campo Santo at Pisa. The monument at Turin.

7. VENICE ADDED TO ITALY in the more recent distress of Austria. Occupation of Rome as the Capital of the Italian Kingdom.

8. THE KINGDOM OF ITALY IN ITS GENERAL CHARACTER. Its material capacities and defects. Political strength given it by the establishment of the new Prussian power. Political difficulties. Religious difficulties. The education question. Hopes for the future.

SPAIN.

FIRST LECTURE.

THE PERIOD OF GROWTH AND STRENGTH.

1. SOURCES OF INFORMATION regarding growth and decay of the Spanish power.   Peculiar value of the investigation of the general course of Spanish history.   .

2. PHYSICAL ADVANTAGES OF SPAIN, as regards commerce, manufactures, etc.   Examination of Buckle's statement regarding effects of physical causes on the Spanish national character.

3. EARLY HISTORY OF SPAIN.   The mixture of Roman, Barbarian, Christian and Mohammedan elements.   The religious wars.   Liberties of municipalities and districts.   The Church.   Some leading characteristics of the nation.

4. Ferdinand and Isabella.   Union of territories.   Centralization of power.   Alliance with the Church made closer. The Inquisition.   Religious wars renewed.   Expulsion of the Jews.   The statesmanship of Ximenes.   Effects of colonial. mines.   Ranke's view.

5. CHARLES I. (Charles V. of Germany).   Concentration of power in him.   The main cause of his difficulties with Spain. Insurrections.   Use made of them in suppressing remains of old Spanish liberties.   Buckle's observations on character of wars prosecuted by Charles, two out of three being wars of religion.   His resistance to the Papacy in temporal, but support in spiritual matters.   Evidence of this in his last years, and in the codicil to his will.   Effect of his reign on the nation, and on the Spanish character.

6. PHILIP II.   Difference between Charles and Philip in relation to Spain, and to Europe.   His strength among the people, and in Europe.   Macaulay's statement of this, and of the extent and power of Spain at this period.   Acquisition of Portugal.   The leading features of his foreign policy. Part taken in the wars of religion in France.   Marriage in

England. War against England. War with the Netherlands. Domestic policy. War with the Moriscos. The Inquisition. Ancient and modern arguments and apologies for the Inquisition. Balmes's argument. Lafuerte. Dalton (cite preface to Hefele's Ximenes). Philip's resistance to Papacy in certain temporal matters. His zeal in spiritual matters. His conscientiousness and vigor. Germs planted and fostered by him.

SPAIN.

SECOND LECTURE.

THE PERIOD OF DECLINE.

1. RAPIDITY AND EXTENT OF THIS DECLINE.   Various statements and explanations of it: Sempere's; Dunham's; Buckle's.

2. PHILIP III.   Twenty years rule of the Duke of Lerma. Close alliance with the Church.   Increase in ecclesiastical influence, and in religious foundations.   The Archbishop of Valencia, and the expulsion of the Moriscos.   Effect of their expulsion.   Their services to Spain in agriculture, manufactures, etc.   The Netherlands independent.

3. PHILIP IV.   Rule of the favorite Olivares.   Pretenses of reform.   Decline in national industry.   Insurrection of the Catalans.   Rebellion in Portugal.   Loss of West India trade. Loss of revenue and strength at home, and of consideration abroad.

4. CHARLES II.   His wretched condition, physical and mental.   Power of the Church.   Condition of trade, manufactures, municipal wealth, army and navy, etc.   Intrigue for the succession.   Porto Carrero.

5. PHILIP V.   Accession of the Bourbons.   War of the Succession.   Revival of Spain.   Disappearance of Spanish talent.   Foreign skill called into army, schools, manufactures, mines, diplomacy, finance, and even supreme management of state affairs.   Vendome, Alberoni, Ripperda, and others.   Restraint on the Church.

6. FERDINAND VI.   Progress in Spanish affairs.   Restraint of the Church.   Improvement of revenue.   Treasure left to his successor.

SPAIN.

THIRD LECTURE.

PERIOD OF DECLINE.

1. CHARLES III. Sources of his ideas. Domestic policy. Freedom of trade; law-reform; education; public works; literature and science. Dealing with banditti. His ministers, Campomanes and Aranda. Policy as to Church. Practical suppression of the Inquisition. Expulsion of the Jesuits. Restriction of pecuniary tributes to Rome. Colonial policy. Growth of Spain and new colonies under it. Comparison with cotemporary policy of England. Foreign policy. Position of Spain in Europe. Treaties with infidel powers.

2. CHARLES IV. Reaction. Undoing in five years the work of three generations of statesmen. Restoration of power to Church, and of energy to the Inquisition. Aid to American colonies against England. Rapid sinking of Spain. Godoy. Spain at the coming in of the French Revolution. Treaty of Basle (1795). The Crown Prince and Escoiquiz. Napoleon's snare. Seizure and imprisonment of Spanish royal family.

3. JOSEPH BONAPARTE. His attempt at just rule. Reforms. His misgivings. Spanish uprising. Character of the war of Spanish liberation. Loss of the American colonies.

4. FERDINAND VII. The restoration of the Spanish Bourbons. Reaction. Inquisition. *Index Expurgatorius.* Expulsion of professors. Revolution of 1821. Riego. Final abolition of Inquisition. Conference of Verona, and interference by the Holy Alliance. Duke of Angouleme's expedition. Insurrections, confusions and distress. Change in law of succession. Blanco White's picture of Spain.

5. ISABELLA II. War of the succession. Christina and Don Carlos. Intrigues, pronunciamentos, insurrections and revolutions. French marriage intrigues. Queen's religion and morality. Revolutions and counter-revolutions. Final overthrow of Isabella.

6. INTERREGNUM. General Prim. Victor Amadeus. Difficulties. The Savoy tradition, and the King's lessons to Spain. Mr. John Hay's vivid picture of recent Spanish affairs. The abdication of Victor Amadeus; its causes and results. Castellar, the republic, and the reaction.

7. SUMMARY OF MAIN CAUSES OF SPANISH DECLINE: A. The religious wars, the spirit which generated them and was generated by them. B. Persecution and the Inquisition. C. Expulsion of the Jews and Moriscos. D. Power given the Church, and growth of clerical body. E. Feeling regarding commerce and manufactures. F. Anarchic tendencies. Resumption of all these into one statement by Buckle. Relation in Spain between government and people.

AUSTRIA.
FIRST LECTURE.

1. The Breaking up of Mediæval Institutions, at the close of the Fifteenth Century. Favorable characteristics of Maximilian for taking part in this extension of Austrian power. The Burgundian marriage, and others. Consolidation of Austrian power. The Landpeace and Imperial Council. Improvement in military organization. Improvement in general civilization. Interesting change in theory of empire at this period. (Comparison between Pütter and Bryce).

2. The Reformation Period. Charles V. and his power. His characteristics. His wars and general work. Effects of the Reformation on the monarchy, and on the political condition of the empire. The religious peace of Passau, 1552 (or Augsburg, 1555).

3. The Toleration Period. Division of the realm of Charles V. at his death. Accession of Ferdinand I. Good effects of the "Religious Peace." Ferdinand's noble adherence to toleration. His difficulties. Adherence of sundry other German emperors to toleration, especially Maximilian II., for over sixty years.

4. Period of the Thirty Years War. Difficulties in the way of toleration. Ferdinand II. and his bigotry. Corresponding bigotry on the Protestant side. Evangelical Union, and Catholic League. Terrible material and moral results. Wretched political results. Peace of Westphalia (1648).

5. Period of Advancement. A. Sufferings and indignities from Louis XIV. Consolation finally from Prince Eugene. B. Sufferings and indignities from the Turks. Redemption by John Sobieski. C. Sufferings and indignities from Frederic the Great, Prussia and Bavaria. Aid from the Hungarians.

6. Period of Recovery. Rule of Maria Theresa. Circumstances of her accession. Fusion of Hungary into Germany. The Partition of Poland, and the judgments which have been passed upon it.

AUSTRIA.

SECOND LECTURE.

THE REIGN OF JOSEPH II., 1780-90.

1. IMPORTANCE OF THIS REIGN in the study of political and social progress.

2. CHARACTER OF THE GERMAN IMPERIAL MONARCHY when Joseph began his work. Its extent. Its subjects. Diversity of origins, customs, languages and ideas. Power of nobility and clergy.

3. EDUCATION OF JOSEPH. His travels. Influence direct and indirect upon his ideas. His life before his accession to full imperial power. Comparison of his liberalism with that of Frederic the Great.

4. JOSEPH'S THEORIES OF REFORM: A. As to Consolidation of Empire; B. as to Feudalism; C. as to Superstition and Ecclesiastical Dominion; D. as to Advancement of thought; E. as to building up Material Interests.

5. JOSEPH'S PRACTICE IN REFORM: A. *Consolidation of Empire.* Difficulties. Resistance. Example of this in Hungary. B. *Dealings with Feudalism.* Edict of 1780. Abolition of corvees, heriots, etc. Greatest defect in this. Example given by England and Russia on this point. Joseph's remark about equality. C. *Dealings with the Church.* Blow at Papal intrusion. Suppression of monasteries. Provision for secularized education. Effects of this attempt in the Netherlands. Suppression of monasteries, pilgrimages, and sundry fetichisms. Edict of toleration. Good treatment of Protestants and Jews. Abolition of clerical censorship. D. *Efforts for Advancement of Thought.* Difference between Joseph II. and Frederic the Great in literary culture. Comparison of their work. Joseph's creation of schools, colleges and universities. E. *Efforts for Advancement of Material Interests.* Aid to manufactures. Suppression of internal customhouses. Prohibitory duties. Canals, roads, harbors, etc. Efforts to open navigation of the Scheldt.

6. JOSEPH'S DEALINGS WITH THE NETHERLANDS' CHARTER. *La Joyeuse Entrée.* His competition in education with the clerical establishment at Louvain. Rebellion. Declaration of independence.

7. JOSEPH'S DEALINGS WITH HUNGARY. Superstition regarding Poland and Hungary recently current among us. Difficulty in combating these. Joseph's dealings with the nobility. His compromise.

8. JOSEPH'S MINISTERS. Kaunitz and his brood. Summary. Excellences and defects of Joseph's character and method. What was lost and what remained. His epitaph.

AUSTRIA.

THIRD LECTURE.

FROM DEATH OF JOSEPH TO REVOLUTION OF 1848.

1. REACTIONARY DEVELOPMENT OF AUSTRIAN STATESMANSHIP. Kaunitz, Thugut, Colloredo, Cobentzl, Metternich. The Camarilla's influence.

2. THE UNDOING OF REFORM. Leopold II. His character and previous history. Influences brought to bear upon him. His concessions in Church and State.

3. DEALINGS WITH THE FRENCH REVOLUTION. The Declaration of Pilnitz. Alliance and distrust between Austria and Prussia. Murder of the French ambassadors at Rastadt. Feebleness of the Austrian method of conducting the war against France. Treachery of Thugut in military calamities. Moreau, Pichegru and Jourdan in north ; Bonaparte in south. Treaty of Campo Formio.

4. DEALINGS WITH NAPOLEON. Recuperation of Austrian power. Causes of this. Catastrophe of Marengo, and treaty of Luneville. Ulm, Austerlitz, and treaty of Presburg. Wagram, and treaty of Vienna. Descent of Austria shown in these treaties. Downfall of German empire, and creation of empire of Austria. Austria turned against Russia. Extrication by Metternich. The masterpiece of his school of statesmanship.

5. THE REACTION AFTER NAPOLEON'S DOWNFALL. The Holy Alliance. Its results in Austria, in Italy, in Europe at large. Character of Francis I. of Austria. Increasing discontent. Double insurrection in Gallicia (1846). Its effects in strengthening reaction.

AUSTRIA.
FOURTH LECTURE.
FROM 1848 TO THE PRESENT TIME.

1. REVOLUTION OF 1848. Shock given to Austria. In-surrections in Vienna and elsewhere. Dangers revealed in Germany at large. Most startling revelation of all—want of national unity; in Hungary. Straits of the empire. Russian intervention. Abdication of Francis II. and accession of Francis Joseph.

2. THE SECOND REACTION. New power of the Camarilla and Jesuits. Passiveness of the new emperor. Repressive measures. New Concordate. Apparent success in victories over new Italian spirit. Austrian brutality in Italy. The awakening at the Italian war of 1857. New revelation of Austrian weakness. Wretched condition of finances.

3. THE NEW PATH OF AUSTRIAN STATESMANSHIP. Lessons it has learned: as to clerical supremacy; as to dealings with her various nationalities; as to finances; as to progress in liberty and education. (Effect of lesson learned in its intrigues with France, as to Mexican empire; and in war with Prussia, 1869; and in dealings with Italy). The new brood of statesmen. Buol, Beust, Andreassy, and others. The Austro-Hungarian monarchy. Hopeful indications. Recent material progress. Growth of the Austrian capital. Public enterprise. Extension of railways; industrial enterprises. Significance of the Exposition of 1873. Relations of Government to the Church.

THE NETHERLANDS.

FIRST LECTURE.

1. PLACE OF THE HISTORY OF THE NETHERLANDS in Universal History. Physical characteristics. Development of certain mental and moral characteristics during the Middle Ages. Bravery. Industry. Thrift. Impatience of Tyranny. Van Artevelde as a type. Turbulence. Feuds of "Hooks," and "Cods."

2. THE BURGUNDIAN SOVEREIGNTY. Its extent, power, brilliancy, manufactures and commerce. Growth of cities. Growth of rights and laws. Architecture. The Town Halls and their meaning. Painting. Political and social life as revealed by Froissart ; by Walter Scott ; by Barante.

3. DIFFERENCES BETWEEN NORTHERN AND SOUTHERN PROVINCES in certain popular characteristics, and in peculiarities of growth. Holland brought under Burgundian power (1428). Reign of Philip the Good. Extension of Municipal Liberties. Charles the Bold and his struggle with Democracy ; and his resistance to the Centralization of Power.

4. THE TRANSFER TO THE HOUSE OF AUSTRIA, and to Spain. Mary of Burgundy. Maximilian of Austria. Philip. Charles II. of Burgundy (Charles I. of Spain and V. of Germany).

5. THE PROTESTANT REFORMATION. Circumstances favorable to its adoption and spread in the Netherlands. First persecutions by Charles. The great European wars and their effect on this persecution. New incentives to intolerance. Anabaptists. Fanaticism. Repressive measures. Popular development during this period. Abdication of Charles.

6. ACCESSION OF PHILIP III. OF BURGUNDY (Philip II. of Spain). Philip in the Netherlands. His energy against heresy. Mingled religious, political and personal motives. Inquisition. New bishops. Stringent policy. Philip's departure, and rule from Spain. Regency of Duchess of Parma. Granville.

7. "LE COMPROMIS DES NOBLES" (1566). The Gueux. Political and religious causes of war. Alva. Terror at his approach. His administration. Egmont and Hoorn. Value of their example then and since. (Rossel's posthumous works). The Prince of Orange. Departure of Alva. General state of the Netherlands. The pictures of Cardinal Bentivoglio's History compared with those of Schiller, Motley, and Davies.

8. THE FINAL STRUGGLE AGAINST SPANISH RULE. Requesens and his successors. Don John of Austria. Viglius. Popular spirit. Siege of Leyden. "Spanish fury" at Antwerp. Pacification of Ghent. Foundation of the University at Leyden. The union of Utrecht (1579). Foundation of the Republic of the Seven Provinces.

THE NETHERLANDS.
SECOND LECTURE.

FROM THE UNION OF UTRECHT (1579) *TO THE TREATY OF MUNSTER (WESTPHALIA)* (1648).

1. RENUNCIATION OF ALLEGIANCE TO PHILIP II. by the States General. "The Justification" of the Prince of Orange. Leading characteristics of the resulting war; its bitterness; its complications. Assassination of the Prince of Orange.

2. FOREIGN INTERFERENCE IN THE WAR. Part taken by England. The Earl of Leicester and Sir Philip Sidney; what each sought and found. French interference : The Duke of Anjou at Antwerp, and the " French fury." Henry IV.

3. GROWTH OF STATESMEN. The Family of Orange. Barneveldt. Grotius. Solidity and value of Dutch training in state craft.

4. CONTRASTED EFFECTS OF THE LONG WAR and accompanying events on Holland and Spain. Bankruptcy of Spain. Weakening of Philip II. in power. His death. Summary of his dealings with the Netherlands. Rapid decline of Spain under Philip III. Continuance of the war. The truce of Twelve Years (1609). Recognition of the States General among European powers.

5. A NEW COMPLICATION. Doctrinal differences between Dutch Protestants. Arminius and Gomarus. " Remonstrants" and "Contra-Remonstrants." Bitterness of the struggle. Thoughtful efforts of Dutch statesmen. Action of the clergy. Interference by James of England. Political difficulty complicated with religious difficulty. Maurice, Prince of Orange, and Barneveldt. Arrest of Barneveldt and Grotius. Political operations of Maurice. THE SYNOD OF DORT (1618). Disputes and judgments. Persecution and banishment of leading Remonstrants. Trial and execution of Barneveldt. Bitterness of popular feeling against the Remonstrants. Application of Balmes's theory to these events.

Their importance in the history of progress towards toleration. Escape of Grotius ; his sufferings and triumphs.

6. NEW OUTBREAK OF WAR WITH SPAIN. Varying for-
tunes of the war. Its complication with the Thirty Years
War in Germany. THE TREATY OF MUNSTER (1648). General observations on this struggle of sixty-eight years between the Netherlands and Spain.

THE NETHERLANDS.
THIRD LECTURE.

1. SERIES OF STRUGGLES WITH ENGLAND. Main Causes. Commercial rivalry. Struggle in the colonies. Relations of the House of Orange to the Stuarts. Interference of the States General to save the life of Charles I. Dorislaus's assassination. Treatment of "regicide" embassadors. The English Navigation Act (1651). The war by sea. Dutch bravery. Van Tromp. Cromwell's strength against the Dutch. Blake. Ill-feeling of Charles II. toward the Dutch. Humiliation of England by Dutch after the Restoration.

2. SERIES OF STRUGGLES WITH FRANCE. Invasion of Holland by Louis XIV. Statesmanship of Sir William Temple and John De Witt. Macaulay's sketch of their work. The Triple Alliance (England, Holland and Sweden, 1668). Peace of Aix-la-Chapelle.

3. THE STRUGGLE WITH ENGLAND AND FRANCE UNITED. England seduced from the alliance by France. Charles II. and Louis XIV. Contemptible part taken by the English government. Patriotic sacrifices of the Dutch in resisting this combination. Services of John De Witt. Hatred of Charles II., Louis XIV. and the Dutch rabble concentrated upon him. His murder by the latter. The judgment of mankind upon him then and now. Rise of William of Orange. The country in his hands. His statesmanship and generalship. His invasion of England, acceptance of the British Crown, and dissolution of the French-English alliance (1688).

4. HOLLAND AS A LEADING EUROPEAN POWER. Her union with England and the Continental Allies during the reigns of William and Mary, and Anne, (1688-1714). Peace of Utrecht (1713).

5. HOLLAND IN HER DECLINE. Increase of wealth, but decline in energy. Weakness and loss of colonies. Decline of commerce. Growth of factions. Constitution of 1747. Orange party in full power, and Prince of Orange Stadtholder. Bitter partisanship. Weakness at the outbreak of the French Revolution in 1789.

THE NETHERLANDS.

FOURTH LECTURE.

GENERAL HISTORY OF CIVILIZATION during the Republican Period. Guizot's question and comparison as to French and Dutch Civilization. Doubts as to the justice of his conclusion.

1. INDUSTRIAL AND COMMERCIAL PROGRESS. Development of peaceful activity and power. Great growth of manufactures and commerce. Foreign discoveries and enterprises. Agricultural .progress. Public Works. Drainage ; Beemster Lake and others. Financial institutions.

2. INTELLECTUAL PROGRESS. Institutions of learning. Growth of Literature, Science and the Arts. Inventions— telescope, telegraph, etc. Certain abnormal phases (Tulipomania, etc.)

5. POLITICAL PROGRESS. General character of the government. Leading features in its structure. Effects of predominance of the mercantile· spirit. Blots on the statute books, etc.

4. MORAL PROGRESS. Noble examples of certain Dutch citizens. General reputation of the people. Injuries to this arising from the over-development of the mercantile spirit.

5. MAIN DISTINCTION BETWEEN DIFFERENT PARTS of the Netherlands. General statement of the nature and causes of this difference.

6. THE PERIOD OF DECLINE. Financial difficulties. War debt. Mississippi and South Sea Bubbles. Colonial decay. Decline of commerce. Recurring wars with France, and their effects. The Constitution of 1747. Prince of Orange Stadtholder. Political decline. Results of unrestrained partisanship. The Orange and Patriot parties. Success of the former. Effects of the decay of boldness with the increase of wealth. Weakness of Netherlands in hands of France. Revolutionists and Napoleon.

THE NETHERLANDS.

FIFTH LECTURE.

FROM 1789 TO 1830.

1. Dealings of the French Revolutionary Power with the Netherlands. Invasion of Holland (1793). Patriot party favors the French. Difference between the Dutch resistance to this invasion and to that of Louis XIV. Dissolving power of French philosophy and revolutionary ideas. The Netherlands at the mercy of France. French spoliations.

2. The Netherlands under Napoleon. His cutting and carving at the Belgian provinces. Holland given to Louis Bonaparte as King. Difference between the two brothers as to the theory and practice of government, and its results.

3. The Netherlands from 1815 to 1830. Belgium and Holland united by the treaties of 1815 into a kingdom under the House of Orange. General political intention in this. Difficulties besetting the new kingdom. Differences in religion; tradition; customs; language; interests. Numerical difference. Policy of the Dutch king on each of these points. Suppression of trial by jury. Centralization of administration at the Dutch capital. Dutch monopoly of offices. Laws regarding education abroad. Interference with the ecclesiastical monopoly of the University of Louvain. (Parallel with the attempt of Joseph II.) Conduct of clergy on both sides. Union of ultra liberals with reactionists. Effect on Netherlands of the French revolution of 1830. Revolution at Brussels.

THE NETHERLANDS.
SIXTH LECTURE.
FROM 1830 TO 1874.

1. BELGIUM THROWS OFF ITS ALLEGIANCE to the Nether-lands government. Paralysis of the parties to the treaties of 1815 by the French revolution of 1830. Separation of the two kingdoms. Leopold of Saxe-Coburg made King of the Belgians.

2. HOLLAND SINCE 1830. Agricultural, industrial and eco-nomical progress. Political quiet. Her dangers, real and supposed from Prussia. Good signs in her present condition.

3. BELGIUM SINCE 1830. Thoroughness of her Agriculture. The *Pays de Waes.* Application of Science to Agriculture, and its results. Great development of Manufacturing indus-try; Cockerell at Scraing as a type. Growth and strength of ecclesiastical power. Outgrowth of this in Belgian politics. General development of Belgian people. Importance of Bel-gium in the history of social problems. Mr. Cliffe-Leslie's essays; his comparison of Belgian with English peasantry. Scars left on the nation by Spanish tyranny. Genius in polit-ical common sense shown by Leopold I. His dealings with Revolution. Present political status of the kingdom. Its religious status.

PRUSSIA.

FIRST LECTURE.

THE FOUNDATIONS.

1. BRANDENBURG. A. National characteristics. Disadvantages as to soil, climate, coast. B. Political characteristics —favorable and unfavorable. C. Early history. Turbulence of North German feudal nobles. Emperor Sigismund's appointment of the first Margrave. Character of the family thus introduced, and of its measures. D. Introduction of the Roman law in Sixteenth Century (Savigny). Significance of this. Results. E. Brandenburg in the Renaissance period. F. Brandenburg in the Reformation. Devotion to the new movement. G. Brandenburg in the Thirty Years War. The Calvinist and Lutheran squabbles, and their results. Brandenburg between Tilly and Gustavus Adolphus.

2. PRUSSIA. A. Natural and political advantages and disadvantages. B. Early history. The Teutonic order. Its work in the north. Marienburg and Königsberg. Subjection to Poland. Separation from Poland and union with Brandenburg.

3. THE CONSOLIDATED PRUSSIAN TERRITORY. A. Summary of its characteristics. Effect on its policy of the predominance of disadvantages, natural and political. Happy results.

4. THE GREAT ELECTOR. A. His internal policy. Consolidation of power under him. Wretchedness of the people at large after the Thirty Years War. General administrative policy. The army. Legal reforms. Internal improvements. The Founding of Universities. B. His external policy. His difficulties. Early relations with Sweden, Poland and the Empire. Sturdiness against Louis XIV. Protection of oppressed Protestants. The less satisfactory side of his policy. Explanation.

5. ESTABLISHMENT OF THE PRUSSIAN KINGDOM. Frederic I. Use of him as a foil for the display of Frederic the

Great.   Ridiculous and respectable sides of his effort.   Spirit
shown at his coronation.   Continuance of a large policy regarding education, and learned men by King and Queen.
Importance of this.   Frederic William II.   Peculiar phase of
despotism developed under him.   Comparison of this with
the despotism of Louis XIV.   His whims.   His unloveliness
as depicted by the Margravine of Bareith.   Estimate of him
by Macaulay, Carlyle, and a noted German theologian.   His
steady adherence to the traditional policy of his house.
Steady progress of Prussia under him.

PRUSSIA.
SECOND LECTURE.
FREDERIC THE GREAT.

1. HIS EARLY TRAINING. Conflicting systems and ideas in which he found himself. Early triumph of French ideas in his mind. Later modification of them by the family ideas and traditions.

2. DEVELOPMENT OF FREDERIC'S PHILOSOPHICAL AND LITERARY IDEAS. Influence of the philosophers of the Eighteenth Century upon him. Citations from his philosophic writings; from his attempts in pure literature; from his satirical efforts.

3. DEVELOPMENT OF MILITARY SKILL IN HIM. His first war in Silesia (1740). Its pretext and real cause. Macaulay's sketch of this and other wars of the time. The Seven Years War, and the coalition against him. Disasters and successes. The battle of Rosbach. Personal characteristics exhibited. Wretchedness to which the kingdom was reduced. Turn of fortune in his favor. Results.

4. HIS INTERNAL POLICY. A. Toleration. Relation to Catholics and Protestants, Jesuits, Calvinists, Lutherans, Hussites, Huguenots. Part taken by him regarding Jesuit expulsion. Dealings with Catholic and Protestant persecutors. Common sense in tempering despotism. (Cite Lord Mahon's History and notes). B. Legal reforms. C. Industrial development. D. Sumptuary ideas.

5. PERSONAL CHARACTERISTICS. Strange contradictions in him of cynicism and care for others; of despotism and freedom; of justice and injustice; prodigality and frugality; culture and boorishness. FOREIGN POLICY. Machiavellianism. Macaulay's remark on the contrast between the Anti-Machiavel, and Frederic's entire practice in state-craft. Apparent necessity for this policy. Good results at first. Wretched and ruinous results at a later period.

6. GENERAL RESULTS OF FREDERIC'S REIGN in Prussia. Carlyle's theory. Häusser *vs.* Macaulay. Advance in institutions. Growth of literature. Advance in certain fruitful and dangerous new ideas. General loosening up of old ideas. Various signs of this. Secret societies.

PRUSSIA.
THIRD LECTURE.

1. CONDITION OF NORTH GERMANY just before the beginning of the French Revolution. A. Organization of the various sovereignties. Antiquated laws. Legalized oppression. Abuses. B. Character of the ruling classes. Extravagance and debauchery of the Prince-Bishops and their satellites of the old Church. Pedantry, stiffness and deadness of the Lutheran Church. D. Condition of the people. Destruction of the old barriers between them and oppression. Serfdom.

2. SPREAD OF DISORGANIZING IDEAS. A. French philosophic ideas among the upper classes. Frederic the Great as a type. Effects on government. Effects in producing reforms. Gallomania in literature. B. Among the middle and lower classes. Growth of secret associations. The *Illuminati* Knigge, Weishaupt, and others. Rise of Revolutionists. Feeling of the North Germans toward the first French Republican army, as pictured in Erckmann-Chatrian's novels.

3. CONDITION OF PRUSSIA AT OUTBREAK OF FRENCH REVOLUTION. Reign of Fred. William II. (1786–97). Better state of things in Prussia than in some neighboring States. Worthless character of Fred. William. Decline of nation under him.

4. PRUSSIAN DEALINGS WITH THE REVOLUTION. Counsels of leading German statesmen. Hertzberg. Kaunitz. Disregard of these counsels by Prussia and Austria. Conference and Declaration of Pilnitz. War. Brunswick manifesto. First success but final failure. German jealousies. Partition of Poland. Languor in war. Treaty of Basle (1795). Prussian Machiavellianism and the desertion of Austria. First fruits. Accession of Fred. William III. (1797–1840).

5. PRUSSIAN DEALINGS WITH NAPOLEON. Continuance of Prussian Machiavellianism. Mistake in diplomacy. Mistake in patriotism. Remarks on Johann Von Müller's idea and on recent denunciation of him. Goethe and the new

German literature.   Progress of Napoleon.   Misgivings of
Prussia.   Hardenburg and Haugwitz.   Confederation of the
Rhine.   North German Confederation pretense.   The Han-
over bait.   Degradation of Prussia.   Lowest point in her his-
tory.   Violation of territory.   Declaration of war.   Jena
(1806).   Prostration of Prussia.   Further humiliations.
Treaty of Tilsit (1807).   Results of her Machiavellianism.
Diminution of territory.   Subordination to French schemes.
Her part in the Moscow campaign.   The retreat, and General
Yorck's course.   Conference of Kalisch.

PRUSSIA.

FOURTH LECTURE.

FROM THE GREAT UPRISING IN 1813 TO 1848.

1. RESULT OF THE KALISCH CONFERENCE. King's proclamation. Diplomatic arrangements for a union of the oppressed nations.

2. THE PEOPLE. The statesmanship of Stein. Growth of patriotic feeling. Patriotic gifts. Growth of a new literature. Arndt. Körner. Splendor of the period.

3. THE STRUGGLE. Preparatory efforts of Stein and Scharnhorst. New military creations. New military spirit. Blücher. Battle of Lutzen and Bautzen. Battle of the nations, Leipzig, (1813). March on France. Prussian part in the first restoration of the Bourbons. Balzac's curious statement regarding Blücher's idea of policy. Comparison with saying attributed to Bismarck regarding Paris. Prussian part in battle of Waterloo, and in the Holy Alliance.

4. BEGINNINGS OF PRUSSIAN RECOVERY. Effects of revolutionary efforts. Reaction. Dealings of Fred. William III. with constitutional ideas. His hesitation and double dealing. His dealings with the religious differences of the people. Bigotry shown in opposition. Comparison with history of Holland in this particular. Difficulty of rapid advance under Fred. William III. Vivid remembrances of Revolutionary Period.

5. ACCESSION OF FRED. WILLIAM IV. (1840). His good qualities. Religious tendencies. Scholarly and artistic feeling.

6. POLITICAL PROGRESS. Constitutional growth. Justice and liberal parties. Efforts of close relations of court with Russia and England.

7. RELIGIOUS RELATIONS. Pietism. Beautiful growth of charitable institutions. Slow growth of full toleration. Treatment of the Baptists in Berlin.

8. INTELLECTUAL PROGRESS. The system of general education. The Real Schulen. The gymnasiums. The universities. Free system adopted in them. Intellectual liberty. The new brood of scholars. Temptation to subserviency. Fearlessness of many. Brilliant intellectual growth.

9. MATERIAL GROWTH. Growth of great modern industries. Krupp and Borsig as types. The railway system. The rise of industrial centres. Trade and manufactures. Effects of abolition of commercial restrictions between North German States. Splendid public works. The Rhine Bridges.

10. THE GROWTH OF ART. The collections at Berlin. Public monuments. New museums. Rath-haus. Monument to Frederic the Great, and others. The completion of Cologne Cathedral, and other enterprises. Rauch, Kaulbach, Cornelius, Schwanthaler, Schadow, Danneke, and others.

11. THE GROWTH OF LITERATURE. Fallow time after Goethe, Schiller, and the great writers of the beginning of the century. Good and healthy character of literature of this period.

PRUSSIA.

FIFTH LECTURE.

FROM REVOLUTION OF 1848 *TO CLOSE OF WAR WITH FRANCE,*
(1872).

1. GROWTH OF FEELING IN PRUSSIA FOR CONSTITUTIONAL LIBERTY. Effects of absurd provocations to this spirit.

2. GROWTH OF FEELING FOR NATIONAL UNITY. Difficulties in the character of Fred. William IV., and in the unpopularity of Prussia and Prussians in the other German States. (Reminiscences).

3. EFFECTS IN PRUSSIA OF FRENCH REVOLUTION OF 1848. Outbreak in Berlin. The students. Course pursued by King. Spirit of the Prince of Prussia (the present Emperor, 1872). Wretched results of the German revolution. Waste of effort in the deliberative bodies at Berlin and Frankfort. Half-refusal of the Imperial Crown by Prussian King. Reactionary measures. Withdrawal of constitutional concessions.

4. EXTERIOR RELATIONS. Policy of Prussia during Crimean War. Caricatures in England and France. The truth regarding Prussian policy at that period.

5. DEVELOPMENT OF THE PRUSSIAN SUPREMACY. Accession of William I. Characteristics. First measures as Regent and King. Increasing stringency in military regulations. High tone taken at his coronation. Struggle with Parliament. Bismarck. Danish War, and acquisitions of territory. Great war with Austria. Great victories and acquisitions of territory. Seaports. Strategic points. Commercial consideration gained by Prussia.

6. DEVELOPMENT OF PRUSSIAN MONARCHY into the German Empire. French alarm at Prussian power. Outbreak of war. The pretext. Prussian readiness and French unreadiness. Bismarck and Moltke. Ollivier. Le Boeuf. Thiers's warnings. Conquest of France. Acceptance of the Imperial power by King. Annexation of Alsace and Lorraine. Arguments for and against. The indemnity. Position thus

given the new Empire. Double lesson taught by Prussian success, and its relations to her internal policy. The lesson to Europe as regards intellectual freedom. The lesson to America as regards discipline, thoroughness, and steadiness.

7. STRUGGLE BETWEEN BISMARCK AND THE ROMAN CATH-OLIC CHURCH. Renan's theory of it.

RUSSIA.
FIRST LECTURE.

1. PHYSICAL CHARACTERISTICS OF THE EMPIRE. Comparison of its boundaries at different epochs, on historical maps.

2. BEGINNINGS OF THE EMPIRE. The Republic of Novgorod, and its boast. The tradition of the calling in of Rurik (862). Its significance as an indication of a mixture of Norman and Sclavonic elements.

3. VLADIMIR, and the early religious relations of Russia (1000). Truth probably involved in the traditions. Naturalness of the choice of the Greek Church.

4. THE GROWTH OF CITIES ON RUSSIAN SOIL in the Twelfth Century. The stream of Asiatic commerce in its effects on them.

5. SUBJUGATION OF RUSSIA TO THE MONGOLS (about 1250). Effect of the two centuries of this subjection on Russian character. Anarchy, and Polish wars.

6. IVAN III. (Vasilievitch) (1462–1505). His generalship and statesmanship. Russia wrested from the Mongols. Extension given the empire in all directions. Varied progress. Calling in of European artists and artificers.

7. IVAN IV. (The Terrible) (1533–1584). Difference between first and last parts of his reign. Condition of Russia during his last years. Deepening of Russian loyalty.

8. BORIS GODOUNOFF (1598). His usurpation. Emancipation of the Russian Church from the Greek Patriarchal. Definite and most unfortunate form given to the serf system.

9. PERIOD OF ANARCHY. Pretenders to the throne.

10. THE FIRST ROMANOFF. Election of Michael to the throne. Statesman-like qualities of the first three princes of the present line.

RUSSIA.

SECOND LECTURE.

1. PETER THE GREAT (1682–1725). Condition of Russia as he received it. His training. Ivan and Sophia. The throne in the Kremlin. Lefort.

2. PETER AS A REFORMER. His aims and methods. His career as general, admiral, mechanic, builder, and law-giver. His statesmanship in general. His external policy. Relations with Sweden, Turkey, and Poland. Effects of the French and English civilization of the period on him. His extension of territories. His internal policy. Wonderful character of his creations. His choice of men. His dealings with the Church, Nikon and the Patriarchate. His dealings with the nobles. The Tschin. Its dealings with the serfs. Strengthening of the servile bonds. Over-government. The old Russian party. Alexis, and the attempted reaction. Results.

3. THE FOUR EMPRESSES of the Eighteenth Century in Russia. Comparative nullity of the emperors after Peter's death. *Catharine I.* Effect of her plain sense on Peter. *Anne and Elizabeth.* Degeneracy of autocratic rule under them. The reign of favorites. Biren and his tyranny. Münnich and others. Stagnation in internal affairs. Slow development in diplomatic relations. *Catharine II.* Combination of weakness and strength in her character. Disposition made of her husband, Peter III. Orloff and Potemkin. Internal development of the empire. Foreign standard set up. Relations of Catharine to the Eighteenth Century philosophy and philosophers. Education of her family. Striking surface effects. Slight effect on the people. Type of this in her city building. Remark of Joseph II. External relations. Increasing definiteness of Russian policy. Significance of the new family names. Relations with Turkey; with Germany, and Frederic the Great; with Poland and the last

Polish monarchs; with the French Revolution. General summary of her reign.

PAUL I. (1796–1801). Unfortunate education. Domestic policy. His ideas of prerogative. Ordinary tyranny. Foreign policy. Espousal of anti-revolutionary ideas. Hatred of the French. Welcome to French royal and noble refugees. Sudden revulsion. Paul turns against England, France and Austria. His worship of Bonaparte. The palace intrigue against him. His murder.

RUSSIA.

THIRD LECTURE.

RUSSIA AT BEGINNING OF NINETEENTH CENTURY. Accession of Alexander I. (1800-1825). Remark regarding the statesmen surrounding him at his coronation. His characteristics, and their development. His external policy. His struggle with Bonaparte. Effect of Napoleon's victories upon him. The Treaty of Tilsit. Mixed motives of Alexander. Mixture of elements in his character. Napoleon's saying. Alexander's plans thwarted, and himself deceived by Napoleon. Alexander against Napoleon. Persistency. Effect of burning of Moscow. Alexander's part in the Bourbon restoration in France. His political and religious plans for Europe. Madame de Krudener. The Holy Alliance. Antagonism. Struggle between the old Russia and progressive party. Internal affairs. Cupidity. The old Russian party. Pouchkin's toast. Efforts at reform. How thwarted. His feeling regarding the serf system. His disappointments. Circumstances of his death.

NICHOLAS I. (1825-55). Circumstances of his accession. The great revolt. The efforts of Republicans and doctrinaires. Curious evidence of utter want of political education during this revolt. Nicholas supreme. His character as a man and ruler. His internal administration. Attempts at reform. Internal improvements. How checked by his own fears. His relations to Europe. Character of his influence in Europe. Examples in France, Spain, and Hungary. His dealings with Poland. Successes in Asia, and against Turkey. His use of his ecclesiastical connection in the East. The war in the Crimea. The squabble with France regarding the Holy Sepulchre. Interests of France and England in the East. Remark of the first Napoleon regarding the occupancy of Constantinople. Condition of Turkey. Sevastopol. Nicholas and Sir Hamilton Seymour. Feeling of the English people. Aberdeen. Palmerston. Cobden. The war in the Crimea. Alma, Inkermann, and Sevastopol. Unsuccessful attempt of Russia to bring about a diversion, on the side of the United States. Curious sympathy for Russia of certain classes of Americans. Disappointment, and death of Nicholas.

ALEXANDER II. Speech to the diplomatic corps at his accession. His difficulties. Peace of Paris. Effects of the war on the nation. Alexander Herzen and the " Kolokol." Freedom of the press, and rise of journalism. Reforms. Difficulties. Reforms in telegraphic communication as typical. Primary and other schools. Universities. Struggle for university reform. Disorders. Emancipation of the serfs. Thoroughness and statesmanship of its methods. Feeling of the nobles. Efforts for Constitution. New system of administration of justice. Vigor in internal improvements. The last struggle with Poland. Katkov, and the rousing of Russian patriotism against Poland. Nihilism. General summary of Alexander's work.

RUSSIA.

FOURTH LECTURE.

CIVILIZATION IN RUSSIA (TO THE ACCESSION OF NICHOLAS I).

1. EARLY OBSTACLES IN THE PATH OF RUSSIAN CIVILIZA-TION. Isolation from the main elements of the civilization of Western Europe. A. The Roman spirit in Western Europe, and its absence in the development of Russia. B. The old German spirit in Western Europe, and its absence in the building up of Russia. National and individual character. Lack of Teutonic invasions. Rurik's coming not an exception. Absence of mixture with Teutonic races. Invasions of the Mongols. Effect of the Asiatic spirit. C. The Christian Church. Russia cut off from the western church by creed, ritual, tradition and language.

2. MISERY RESULTING FROM THE EARLY COURSE OF RUSSIAN AFFAIRS.

3. PERMANENT NATIONAL INSTITUTIONS AND CHARAC-TERISTICS thus developed. The Kremlin as typical. Crystallizations of superstition and fetichism. Early Russian art. The architecture of Moscow. Church of St. Basil. Early paintings. Shrines of Tzars and Patriarchs, in the Kremlin. The Tower of Ivan. Palaces of the old Tzars, and light thrown by them on old Russian policy.

4. PETER THE GREAT. Summary of his work. Evidences of his energy at St. Petersburg and Moscow. Peter's great errors, and their existing results. His own government. Its fruits to-day. His depreciation of man as man; results of this in his time and since. Personal observations of my own among serfs, and in the country at large. Effects of Peter's policy on the serfs,—on the serf-owners,—on the country. Summary of good and evil agency of Peter in Russian civilization.

5. CATHARINE II. Good and evil effects of the Eighteenth Century ideas and practices upon her. Change in public estimation of her work.

6. ALEXANDER I. Unfortunate mixture of motives. His difficulties within and without the empire. The old Russian party.

RUSSIA.

FIFTH LECTURE.

CIVILIZATION IN RUSSIA (SECOND PART).

1. THE PROGRESS OF RUSSIA UNDER NICHOLAS. Change from his character in youth to his character as monarch shown by his portraits. Characteristics shown at his accession. His physical courage, and moral timidity. Effect of traditions of French Revolution upon him. Evidences of these in his public improvements; in his church-building, and in dealings with ecclesiastical affairs; and with official corruption. Nicholas's dealings with the serf system. Character of the serfs. Their shrewdness; superstition; blind obedience; kindly qualities. System of serf labor. Personal and crown serfs. Corvee system. Obrok system. Nicholas's steadiness in working towards emancipation. Opposing arguments.

2. NEGATIVE AND POSITIVE ELEMENTS IN NICHOLAS'S CHARACTER. Want of faith in coördination of liberty and order. Faith in despotic methods. His dislike of constitutional liberty. Two striking monuments of this still in the Kremlin: Napoleon's statue, and the dishonored Polish Constitution. Remaining evidences of it in Europe. His popularity. The popularity of Russia at one time among certain classes in the United States. Causes of this. His death.

3. ALEXANDER II. Hopes for Russian civilization under him. His character. His abolition of the serf system. His statesmanlike provision for the freedmen. Relaxation of governmental regulations. Internal improvement. Danger at this moment for the old Russian party.

4. PART TAKEN BY DESPOTISM in the development of Russian civilization. The internal difficulties.

5. PART TAKEN BY THE NOBILITY. Its wealth; its weakness. Display of its inefficiency in Russia, and throughout Europe. One exception: Prince Galitzin, in Pennsylvania.

6. PART TAKEN BY THE CLERGY. Defect in their fundamental ideas. Their unfortunate views of education.

7. PART TAKEN BY THE PEOPLE AT LARGE. Disturbing elements in the provinces on the western frontier. Spirit of their poetry and music. Beggary. Anomalies. Subordination of mental to physical strength. Encouraging features of the great central districts. Good characteristics of the nation. Training of the peasantry by the patriarchal democratic system. Semi-political activity in peasant villages. Effects of the emancipation. Hopes for the Russian people. Lessons from the comparison of Russian with American ideas and institutions.

POLAND.

FIRST LECTURE.

1. CURRENT FALLACIES REGARDING POLISH HISTORY. Peculiar value of its careful study. The works of Chodzko, Salvandy, Rulhière, and others. Light thrown on the progress of Polish history by the study of historical geography.

2. ABSENCE OF THE "ROMANIC ELEMENT" from Polish civilization. Important results. Salvandy's statement regarding the effect of this on representative government. (Salvandy, *Vie de Sobieski*, vol. I., pp. 106–9).

3. THE NOBILITY. Their warlike spirit. Their main idea of liberty. Shape taken by this in the Assembly of Volo, and the *Liberum Veto*. Tenacity regarding this. Views held by nobles regarding commerce and trade. Results: individual; social; and national. Comparison with Spain in this respect.

4. THE POLISH CLERGY. Unfortunate difference between their position and political work in Poland, and in Western Europe.

5. THE PEOPLE. Residents of the towns. Jews; effect of popular ideas upon them. The serfs: causes of their degradation.

6. ATTEMPTS TO BETTER POLISH AFFAIRS. Representative system of 1467. Its wretched defects. Retention of the *Liberum Veto*. Power left in constituencies. Scope to foreign machinations.

7. ADDITIONAL CAUSES OF ANARCHY. The Reformation. Toleration. Lutherans and Socinians.

8. THE POLISH MONARCHY. Early mixture of hereditary and elective principles. The Piasts and Jagellons. Later elective character. Curious results. Henry of Valois and John Sobieski as types. Sobieski's career. Effects of his renown in prolonging the life of the Republic. His attempt at radical reform. Rulhière's account of his letter to Louis

XIV.   The final scene in his attempt at reform.   His speech.
(Salvandy, III., p. 374).

9. DEBASEMENT OF MONARCHY, CLERGY, AND NOBILITY,
and utter contempt for the people, as shown in two typical
cases: The dealings with Poland by Charles XII. of Sweden,
and Catharine II. of Russia.

POLAND.   ·

SECOND LECTURE.

THE PARTITIONS AND FINAL RUIN.

1. EXCUSES FOR FOREIGN INTERVENTION. Polish anarchy and intolerance. Logical progress from intervention to partition. Louis XIV. Feud between greater and lesser nobles. Attempt at reform checked, and " Polish liberties guaranteed " by Russia and Prussia. Secret article in treaty of 1764, as given by Schlosser (*History of the Eighteenth Century*, IV., 383, note). Election of Poniatowski (1764). Russian machinations. Partitions of 1772, '93 and '95. Territorial results of each, as shown on historical maps. General results, immediate and remote, on Europe.

2. THE REVIVAL OF NATIONAL FEELING. Attempts at reform. Constitution of 1791. Toleration. Burghers. Serfs. Monarchy. Opposition by neighboring despots. Uprising after Second Partition (1794). Kosciusko. His first successes and final failure.

3. DEALINGS OF NAPOLEON WITH POLAND. Hopes held out by him to Polish patriotism. Futility and cruelty of these, as shown by Lanfrey. Creation of the Duchy of Warsaw.

4. POLAND AFTER 1815. The Russo-Polish kingdom, and Alexander I. of Russia. Insurrection of 1831. Consequent treatment of Poland by Nicholas. Monument of this in the Kremlin at Moscow. True theory of Russian religious persecutions in Poland. The more recent insurrections. Part taken by Poles in European revolutionary movements. Satire on this in Sardou's *Rabagas*.

THE TURKISH POWER.
FIRST LECTURE.
GROWTH OF THE EMPIRE.

1. APPARENT REMOTENESS, BUT REAL VALUE OF THIS HISTORY. A. Its relations to the early modern history of France and Germany. B. Its relations to the more recent history of Russia, England and France. C. Its general value in a study of political causes and results.

2. BEGINNINGS AND PROGRESS OF THE EMPIRE. Legend of Ertoghrul (Thirteenth Century). Strong character of Osman and his successors. Conquests. Warlike character of the people. Semi-feudal system. The Timarli: Feudal and irregular troops. Organization of a paid standing army. The Spahis of the Porte. The Janissaries (1361). Advance on contemporary military ideas of Europe in this organization. Its origin; spirit; discipline.

3. THE LAST YEARS OF THE OLD EASTERN EMPIRE. A. Its political character. Effects of the Byzantine despotism. Futility of its political expedients. Enervation. Abject attitude toward the Turks, and toward Europe. B. Its religious character. Peculiar development of fetichism and fanaticism. Ecclesiastical separation from Western Europe.

4. THE TURKISH POWER APPROACHING ITS HEIGHT. Its steady progress in subduing the Byzantine Empire. Temporary repulses by European heroes. John of Hunyad. George Castriot (Scanderbeg).

5. THE CONQUEST OF CONSTANTINOPLE (1453). Mohammed II. His great qualities. Main features of his conquest of the city. Thoroughness of his work in establishing Mohammedanism. Toleration of the Greek Church. Comparison between the two religions as they then stood. Leading effects of the taking of Constantinople on European civilization. Extension of the Turkish power over Greece and towards Northern Europe.

6. THE ALARM OF EUROPE. The "Turk's bell." Litanies. Attempted crusades. Efforts of the Popes. Capestrano. General failure of combined opposition. Effects of the clash of military interests between France and Germany on this opposition. Effect of the Reformation. Effect of the mercantile spirit of certain Italian Republics. Hungarian heroism. John of Hunyad's persistence. His repulse of the Turks from Belgrade. Occasional efforts of Venice and Genoa.

7. UNION OF SPIRITUAL AND MILITARY SUPREMACY IN THE SULTANS. Conquest of Syria by Selim I. His succession to the religious heritage of the Caliphs (1517).

8. SUMMARY OF THE MAIN CAUSES OF THE RISE OF THE TURKISH POWER. A. Physical causes. B. Moral causes. Effects of certain doctrines and precepts. Growth of Mohammedan views regarding eastern Christians and Christianity. C. Political causes. Peculiar phase of contemporary European politics.

THE TURKISH POWER.
SECOND LECTURE.

THE EMPIRE AT ITS HEIGHT. BEGINNINGS OF ITS DECLINE.

1. SOLYMAN THE MAGNIFICENT (1520–1565). Galaxy of great contemporaries on the thrones of Europe. Solyman's victories. Belgrade. Rhodes. Mohacs. Repulse from Vienna. Effects of contemporary events in aiding him. His alliance with Francis I. Splendor of his reign, except at its close.

2. EXTENT OF TERRITORIES OF THE EMPIRE AT ITS HEIGHT. A. The Asiatic and African territories. Looseness of their government. B. The European territories: Climate; soil; divisions; people; labor. Slavonians; Roumanians; Greeks; Jews; Armenians. C. Effect of these divisions on the retention of Turkish power. D. The great barriers between the Turkish capital and Europe. The Danube and its fortresses. The Danubian provinces. The Balkan.

3. THE WAR OF TWO HUNDRED YEARS with Germany. Remorseless character of this war. Incentives to ferocity on either side. Generalization upon the various treaties during its continuance. Rise of great generals on the German side. Don John and the battle of Lepanto. Montecuculi and the Fabian policy. John Sobieski and the defense of Vienna. Prince Eugene. Increasing weakness of the Turks. Periods of spasmodic strength. Mohammed IV. and the Vienna expedition as typical.

4. STRUGGLES OF TURKEY with her Asiatic satraps, and with Persia. Results of the former of these. Causes and effects of the latter.

5. STRUGGLES WITH THE ITALIAN REPUBLICS. A. With Genoa. B. With Venice. Temporary success, but final discomfiture of the Republic. The Morea and Candia.

THE TURKISH POWER.
THIRD LECTURE.
CONTINUANCE OF DECLINE.

1. THE HUNDRED YEARS STRUGGLE WITH RUSSIA. Early success and final discomfiture of Peter the Great. His taking of Azov. His loss of it, and narrow escape. Dealings of the Empress Catharine I. and the Grand Vizier on that occasion, as furnishing typical example in the degeneracy of Turkish character.

2. CONTINUANCE OF ANTI-TURKISH POLICY by Russian rulers, especially by Catharine II. New names in the Russian Imperial family. Victories of Suwaroff. Treaties of Kutschuk-Kainardschi and Jassy. Line of the Dniester. Apparent magnanimity of Russia. Her proposed policy. Detaching of the Crimea from Turkey.

3. ENCROACHMENTS OF ALEXANDER I. Treaty of Tilsit. Napoleon's views and expressions. Russia's gain at Treaty of Bucharest (1812). Bessarabia.

4. ENCROACHMENTS OF NICHOLAS I. His first war. Paskievitch and Diebitch. The attack in Asia,—Erivan. The attack in Europe,—Passage of the Balkan. Typical difficulty of the Turks. Treaty of Adrianople. The new gain in Russian policy. Intervention in the Principalities. Nicholas's main opponent; Sir Stratford Canning (Lord Stratford de Radcliffe).

5. THE GRECIAN STRUGGLE FOR INDEPENDENCE. Difficulties of the Western Powers. Destruction of the Turkish fleet at Navarino. Rapid reversal of European fears regarding Turkey.

6. MAHMOUD II. His destruction of the Janissaries. Its results.

7. WAR OF THE CRIMEA. Nicholas of Russia and Sir H. Seymour. "Question of the Holy Sepulchre." Orloff at Constantinople. Lord Stratford de Radcliffe. Part taken by

France, England, Sardinia, Austria, Prussia. Silistria, and
military peculiarities of Turks shown there. Austrian occupation of Principalites. War transferred to the Crimea. De-
based position of Turkish troops after defense of the fortresses. The Alma; Inkermann; Kars; Sevastopol and its
capture. The Treaty of Paris; imperfection of its settlement. Better solution possible. Turkey under Abdul-Assiz.
Decline of English, and revival of Russian influence at Constantinople. Ignatieff. Loss of control in Egypt. Asserted
independence of Servia.

8. GENERAL RECAPITULATION REGARDING TURKISH DE-
CLINE. A. General moral causes; effects of them seen in
reigning family, even before the death of Solyman II.
Worthlessness of most of his successors. Breaking up national feeling. Decline of discipline in the army. Praetorian
spirit. B. Cessation of the infusion of new and Christian
blood. C. Loss of certain particularly valuable nurseries of
soldiers; as the Crimea. D. Successive disasters to its navy.
Lepanto; Navarino; Sinope. E. Destruction of the Janissaries. F. General abnormal character of the whole Turkish
system.

FRANCE.

FIRST LECTURE.

*ESTABLISHMENT OF FRENCH UNITY.—CENTRALIZATION.—BE-
GINNINGS OF INTELLECTUAL RELATIONS IN EUROPE.*

1. SIMILARITY OF POLITICAL CIRCUMSTANCES and tendencies in all European nations in Fifteenth Century. Comparisons.

2. CONDITION OF FRANCE AT CLOSE OF MIDDLE AGES.
Dismemberment and anarchy. The English occupation.
Powers and ideas of nobles. Leagues. Lawlessness. Military system. Uncontrolled soldiery. The people; their
misery. War, pestilence and famine. The Church. Light
thrown by the history of that age on certain ecclesiastical
hopes and promises in this. Character and reign of Charles
VII. (1422–61).

3. THE CENTRALIZATION PROCESS. Struggle for national
existence against the English. Their expulsion. Importance
to Europe and to France of the year 1453. Results of this
struggle. Formation of the first standing army. *Taille* made
perpetual. Creation of new royal courts or parliaments. Beginnings of codes. Improvements in France. (Jacques
Coeur). Dealings with the Church. Questions between
councils and Popes. Pragmatic sanction.

4. REIGN OF LOUIS XI. (1461–83). Efforts of the nobles.
King's struggle against them. Traits shown by him. Philip
de Commines's chronicles. Walter Scott's pictures. Louis's
style of negotiation. Opposition from all sides. " League of
the Public Good." Typical examples in his dealings with
Charles the Bold and the citizens of Liege. His system in
selecting state servants. Extension of power in creation of
royal courts of justice. His dealings with the Church. Cardinal Baluc's case. Contrast between his public and personal
relations to the Church. His agency in general progress.
The Press. The Post. Institutions of learning. Curious

exception in his treatment of sundry books. General summary of his work.

5. CHARLES VIII. (1483–98). Condition of the people, as revealed in the statement of grievances at States General of 1484. Fruitlessness of attempts at reform by that body. Revolts of nobles. The expedition into Italy (1494–98). Important results to Europe. Its effects on diplomatic and international relations. Results on France. Effects on the national character, and on French art. Cause assigned by Guizot for this and similar expeditions at this period.

6. LOUIS XII. (1498–1515). External affairs. Continuance of active interference in Italy. International relations developed on a larger scale. Growth of the idea of the " Balance of Power." League of Cambray, and Holy League. Internal affairs. Growth of royal courts or parliaments ; of better criminal procedure ; of legal profession ; of postal communication ; of art, and especially architecture. Good effect of Louis's personal character on the nation. Evil effects of the personal characteristics of certain French monarchs on French history ; Francis I., Henry IV., and Louis XIV. as examples.

FRANCE.
SECOND LECTURE.
THE RENAISSANCE.

1. INFLUENCES UPON EUROPEAN CULTURE AND THOUGHT at the end of the Fifteenth Century and at the beginning of the Sixteenth.

2. HOW THESE INFLUENCES WERE BROUGHT TO BEAR ON FRANCE. Feeble influence from the German side. Strong influence from the Italian side. Effects of the French military expeditions into Italy about the beginning of the Sixteenth Century.

3. RENAISSANCE ARCHITECTURE in France. Temporary development of beauty. General peculiarities of French structures of this period ; their two main phases. Two grades of Paganism: St. Eustache at Paris, and the Chapel of St. Pierre at Caen, as types of the first; the Chateaux of Anet and Fontainebleau, as types of ths second.

4. RENAISSANCE SCULPTURE. The calling in of foreign sculptors: Benevenuto Cellini. Height attained by French native genius: Jean Goujon.

5. RENAISSANCE PAINTING. Importation of great Italian artists and works. Traditions regarding the respect shown them by Francis I. Legend of the death of Leonardo da Vinci. The reception of Raphael's work.

6. THE PLASTIC ARTS. Bernard Palissy and his work. His real greatness. Continued development of these arts under Henry II.

7. THE NEW SCHOLARSHIP. Erasmus at Paris. Budaeus. Henry Estienne. Dolet. Opposition to the Sorbonne and Scholastics.

8. THE NEW LITERATURE. Marot and Rabelais at its extremes. Opposing tendencies in the literature of this period. Unfortunate result.

9. CHARACTER AND IDEAS OF FRANCIS I. (1515–47) in re-

lation to the New Art and Culture. His influence in stimu-
lating it; his influence in corrupting it. Treatment of Palissy
and Jean Goujon, as revealing the evil side of his influence.

10. CREATION OF THE COURT. Good and evil of this.
Evil results predominant. Effect of this new institution on
the Renaissance. Lesson in regard to the position of wo-
man in civilized society.

FRANCE.

THIRD LECTURE.

THE REFORMATION AND WARS OF RELIGION.

1. COMPARISON OF FRENCH HISTORY at this period with that of Northern Europe on the one hand, and Southern Europe on the other.

2. THE REFORM PARTY IN FRANCE. Lefevre. Faber. Briçonnet. Calvin. Effects of popular discontent in leading many of the poorer rural population into it. Same effect on certain high nobles by supremacy of certain foreign families, as Medici, Guise, and others, at court. Tendencies of certain thoughtful men and women. Margaret of France.

3. THE CHURCH PARTY. The court. Peculiar union of churchmanship and immorality at the court. Position of the King.

4. BEGINNINGS OF GOVERNMENT DEALINGS WITH HETE-RODOXY. Theory at bottom of these. Special examples made by Francis I. The Vaudois. Struggle of King's better instincts with tendencies to persecution, as shown in Berquin's case. The King yields. Death of Berquin. Tortures of supposed sacrilegious enemies of the Church.

5. HENRY II. AND ANNE DUBOURG. Protestant conspiracy of Amboise. Retribution.

6. ATTEMPTS OF PARTIES TO AGREE. Futility of this, as shown at the Colloquy of Poissy. Attempts at toleration. L' Hopital thwarted by fanatics on both sides. Bodin and Castelnau unheeded.

7. OUTBURST OF CIVIL WAR. Party power gets beyond government control. Outrage at Vassy. Retaliations.

8. THE GROWTH OF PARTIES. Natural division at such periods into three factions: I. Leaders and followers of the Catholic party. The Guises. Mixture of motives. Popular element in the party. II. The Huguenot party. Coligny and the Bourbons. III. The Moderate party. The logic of

each of these parties. The "Logic of Events," in producing such parties.

9. UTTER INCAPACITY OF THE VALOIS KINGS to control the struggle. Henry II. Francis II. Charles IX. Henry III. (1547–98). Contemporary views. (Citations from *L'Estoile*, and *Life of Charles IX*). Their wavering between the two extremes. Political motives mixed with religious. Massacre of St. Bartholomew. Its immediate and remote results. Catholic and Protestant judgment of it.

10. WARS OF THE LEAGUE. General spirit of the time. Henry III. and his court. Difficult position of his court between religious, political and personal considerations. His persecution of the Huguenots, and concessions to them. Stimulus applied to the people from the pulpits. "The Sixteen." Curious parallel between some of its methods and those of the Puritans. Aid from reactionary powers abroad. Sympathy of Philip II. Horrors of the religious war. The Guises at the height of their power. The barricades. The Guises assassinated. Assassination of Henry III. Demoralization and disorganization of France.

11. EFFECTS OF THE REFORMATION and wars of religion on the physical condition of the French people; on their intellectual condition; on their moral condition; on their political development. The great want of France.

FRANCE.

FOURTH LECTURE.

HENRY IV.

1. STATE OF FRANCE AFTER THE ASSASSINATION OF HENRY III. Condition of Paris. Doings in the pulpits and convents. Condition of the country at large.

2. THE STRUGGLE OF HENRY AGAINST FORCE. Efforts of the Church; of Spain; of factions. Elements of strength in Henry. His early life. His training. Its first, great result. Montcontour. His general character. Combination in him of various qualities admired or allowed in that phase of civilization. His shrewdness in the massacre period. Legitimacy. Its recognition by his predecessor, and non-recognition by the Church and religionists. His military progress. Arcques and Ivry as typical battles. Wildness of the League in Paris. Religious fanaticism of the dregs of the French populace. Light thrown by these events on recent Parisian history. Executions among the Paris leaguers. Paris taken.

2. THE STRUGGLE AGAINST OPINION. Change wrought in popular feeling. Strange revolution in Parisian sentiment. Henry's personal efforts toward this. His sayings. (On the manufacture of popular sayings for militant rulers in France). His kindly acts. *The Satire Ménippée.* (Citations from the earliest and latest editions). Change wrought in religious feeling. Effect of his coronation. His conversion. Entrance into Paris. Pacification of the country, and peace with Spain. Vervins, 1598.

4. RELIGIOUS POLICY. Religious condition of France. Policy involved in Henry's conversion. His argument upon it. Conditions of the absolution. The absolution ceremony at Rome. Reëstablishment of the Jesuits. Feeling of the Protestants. Duplessis, Mornay and D'Aubigny as types. *The Edict of Nantes.* Peculiarities of guaranties to the Protestants; granting strongholds; dangers of this system.

Comparison of the Edict of Nantes with the Peace of Passau.

5. FOREIGN POLITICAL POLICY. Dealings with the Austrian power. Plans of Henry and Sully for a great new European States system.

6. DOMESTIC POLICY. Mixture in Henry's statesmanship of thoughtfulness and extravagance ; of sympathy for the people and carelessness. Magnanimous treatment of hostile parties and individuals. SULLY. His ideas and reforms ; his financial management ; his special encouragement to agriculture ; theory on which this was based. Olivier des Serres, and his influence on agriculture. Devotion of Henry to manufactures ; beginnings of leading modern branches of French manufacturing industry. Public works ; building ; the last of the cathedrals. Dealings with the nobles. Their exactions and lawlessness. D'Epernon and Biron ; their relations to taxation. Duelling.

7. COLONIAL POLICY. Champlain in America.

8. NEW GROWTH OF FANATICISM. Disappointment at bottom of it. The assassination of Henry by Ravaillac.

POSTSCRIPT TO SYLLABUS.

A. *It may be observed regarding the foregoing Syllabus of Lectures that it lacks completeness, because it omits the History of England. The simple reason for giving the History of the Great Continental Powers and omitting a distinct series of Lectures on England is, that* PROFESSOR GOLDWIN SMITH *has charge of that subject.*

B. *It may also be noted that the series of Lectures on French History, unlike those on the other nations of Europe, stops far short of the modern period. The completion is given in three additional series of Lectures—already prepared and presented to my classes—on* "FRENCH HISTORY FROM RICHELIEU TO THE REVOLUTION;" *on* "THE FRENCH REVOLUTION;" *and on* "FRENCH HISTORY FROM THE REVOLUTION OF 1789 TO 1874."

A. D. W.

www.ingramcontent.com/pod-product-compliance
Lightning Source LLC
Chambersburg PA
CBHW021520090426
42739CB00007B/693